The Lion Book of
Five-Minute Parables

For Susan   C.R.

For Derek and Lee   N.W.

Text copyright © 2008 Charlotte Ryton
Illustrations copyright © 2008 Nadine Wickenden
This edition copyright © 2008 Lion Hudson

The moral rights of the author and illustrator
have been asserted

A Lion Children's Book
an imprint of
Lion Hudson plc
Wilkinson House, Jordan Hill Road,
Oxford OX2 8DR, England
www.lionhudson.com
ISBN 978 0 7459 6012 8

First edition 2008
1 3 5 7 9 10 8 6 4 2 0

Typeset in 18/24 Lapidary 333 BT
Printed and bound in China

The Lion Book of
Five-Minute
Parables

Told by Charlotte Ryton
Illustrated by Nadine Wickenden

LION
CHILDREN'S

Contents

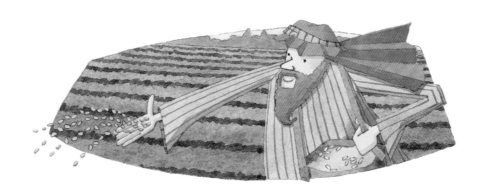

The Sower and the Seed

A story about listening and understanding.

'THERE WAS A sower who went to sow some seed to grow corn for making bread. Up and down the field the sower went, throwing handfuls of seed onto the ground around him. Some of the seed fell onto the path, where the earth was hard. This meant that the seeds did not go into the soil and get covered. Birds hovered in the air above the path as the sower walked along, and then came down and pecked up all the seed.

'Some seed fell on rocky ground, where there was very little earth — just a thin layer of soil over the rocks. The seeds quickly grew into plants but, because the soil was so shallow, their roots had not gone deep enough to get water, so when the sun got very hot they dried up and died.

'And then some seed fell among weeds. The grain started growing into plants, but the weeds grew bigger and stronger and choked the corn so it could not grow.

'But some of the seed fell on good earth. In the good soil, the plants grew strong and produced lots of grain.'

Jesus looked around the crowd to see if they understood what his story meant. 'Listen,' he said, 'and think about what I am saying.'

Later, when Jesus was alone with his disciples, they asked him about his stories. 'Why do you tell the crowds these puzzling stories instead of explaining things in a straightforward way, like you do to us?'

'If I did,' replied Jesus, 'would anyone listen? Everyone likes a story, but only some of them will think about what it means.'

'Well,' said one, frowning in puzzlement. 'What does it mean?'

Jesus explained, 'I am the sower and the seeds are my words. The different types of ground stand for the people who listen to me.

'Now, some people don't really listen at all. My words bounce off them like the seeds on the path. They forget what I've said moments after I've said it.

'And the seeds that fall on stony ground are like the people who

are only half-interested. They hear what I say but they don't think about what it means or do what I say. They are like seed with no roots – so when things get difficult, they give up.

'A third group of people are like the plants choked by weeds. They do listen to me properly but then spend their time making money or having a good time – and so they forget all that I said.

'The last group of people really listen and put my words before everything else – so they grow strong and wise. They try to put my words into action and are able to help others.'

The Rich Fool

Is having lots of money really important?

'RIGHT,' SAID THE man, red in the face with anger, 'let's ask that teacher!' He called out, 'Jesus, I'd like you to decide…'

'Don't listen to him, Jesus,' said another man, who looked a bit like the first. 'My brother just wants me to give him more of the family money.'

'Well, you should,' said the first brother.

'Rubbish,' said the second. 'You're just greedy.'

'Look who's talking…'

Jesus interrupted them. 'I am not a judge. It is not for me to make a ruling about what happens in your family. Go and find a lawyer to sort out your money squabbles.'

Then Jesus turned to the crowd.

'Once, there was a very rich man. He owned a splendid farm with good, fertile land that produced huge harvests. His servants toiled day after day, filling sack after sack with barley.

'"This is wonderful," he said gleefully. But then he began to worry – his barns were almost full.

'"My barn is not big enough for all my crops and all my other possessions as well," he said to himself.

'Then he grinned broadly. "I know what I will do – I will pull down my small barn and build a much, much bigger one. Then I can store all my grain and everything else safely."

'The rich man was very pleased with his plan. He was almost bursting with delight as he watched his new barn's walls get higher and higher, and then watched his servants pack it full with all that his land produced.

' "It is all mine," he gloated as he went into his house and sat down to a splendid meal. "I need never work again. I can sit around eating, drinking and living in luxury."

'As he lay in his soft bed, he imagined the idle life he would lead.

'But in the night he woke to hear God's voice. "You fool! Tonight you will die. And who will have all your grain and possessions then?"

'You see,' Jesus explained, 'that is what will happen to those who pile up riches for themselves but do not do the things that make them rich in God's sight.'

The Great Feast

What happens when God invites you to his party and you say, 'No'.

IT WAS A fantastic meal – all the celebrities had been invited. People outside crowded and strained to see the rich, famous guests arrive. One guest they hoped to see was Jesus.

Jesus sat at the table and said what he was thinking. 'This is a wonderful party, but,' he paused before going on, 'you have only invited people whom you think will give you something in return. What about the poor and the lame and the blind? They can't pay you back. God will invite you to his table in his kingdom if you ask beggars to eat at your table.'

Another guest, wishing to keep the peace, asked Jesus, 'Surely anyone who has a meal in God's kingdom will be blessed?'

Jesus answered him with a story.

'There was once a man who gave a great feast. He invited lots of important people and his best friends.

' "I'll let you know," he told them, "when everything is ready."

'So the servants were ordered to prepare the feast. The cook gathered the finest herbs and most expensive spices to flavour the meat. The kitchen servants chopped and stirred. All over the house and garden, other servants cleaned and polished and swept. When everything was ready, the man sent his servants to all the people he had invited to say, "The feast is ready now, so come and eat and enjoy yourselves."

'But all of them began making excuses.

' "I am so sorry," said the first. "I cannot come as I have just bought a piece of land and must go and see it."

'The second said, "I have just bought some oxen for ploughing and must try them out. Please accept my apologies."

'A third, who was a young man, blushed and said, "I am sorry – I cannot come as I have just got married."

'In the end, none of the people the man had invited came.

'The man was very angry. He told his servant, "Go out into the town. Go into the streets and lanes and ask the poor, and the crippled, the blind and all the beggars to come."

'So the servant went out into the city and asked all the poorest people to come to his master's house for a great feast. Of course, lots of them came, because they were hungry.

'Then the servant told his master, "Sir, I have brought all the people I could find in the city but there is still room for more."

'So his master told him, "Go out into the countryside and tell everyone you see that they simply must come. Invite even the beggars who live in the hedges. I want my house full of people."

'"But," he went on, "none of the people I first invited and who turned me down will get one crumb of my feast."'

The Lost Coin

A story about losing something very precious.

THE HUGE CROWD was silently listening to Jesus telling a story. 'What a load of rubbish,' muttered one old man crossly. 'Look at this crowd lapping it up! A right bunch of villains, they are.'

His friend agreed. 'They wouldn't know the truth if it hit them. Fools and wrongdoers, every one.'

They were right. In the crowd there were men and women who knew they had done things they shouldn't. They had cheated or lied or stolen or been unkind.

'Teacher,' asked one man shyly, 'can even bad people get into God's kingdom?'

Jesus smiled. He knew this man and the bad things he had done. He looked around at the crowd and saw the sad, guilty faces.

'Imagine,' he said. The crowd shifted and made themselves comfortable for the story. 'Imagine a woman who had ten silver coins.'

'A good week's wages,' said the man.

'Exactly – and she needed it all to feed her family. But then something dreadful happened: she lost one of her precious coins.'

Almost everyone in the crowd looked sympathetic. Losing a whole silver coin would be a big problem.

'What do you think she did?'

The answer was obvious. 'She'd look for it, of course!' said someone.

'My mum lost one of her coins,' said a little girl, 'and she got down on her hands and knees to brush the floor, looking for it.'

'Exactly,' said Jesus, smiling down at the eager face looking up

at him. 'She would sweep the whole room very, very carefully and look in every corner. She'd light all the lamps she had so that she would see the coin shining. She'd move any benches or tables to make sure it hadn't rolled under them. And she would go on searching and searching. She would not give up until she found that coin, because it is precious. And when she found it...'

'She'd be really happy,' interrupted the little girl. 'My mum was singing when she found hers.'

'I was so pleased that I asked all my friends round for a party,' added her mother.

'Exactly,' said Jesus. 'God is like that woman. He is really glad when a bad person is sorry for what they have done and turns to him. Everyone in heaven is glad, and the angels in heaven sing with joy.'

Jesus looked round the crowd. The people who looked sad looked much happier now.

'Another peculiar story,' said the cross old man.

But the little girl tugged at Jesus' sleeve and whispered loudly, 'Sir, teacher, tell us another story.'

The Prodigal Son

A story about how God treats sinners.

'ONCE,' SAID JESUS, 'there was a rich farmer who had two sons. When they had grown up, the younger son wanted to move away and not do the mucky, hard work on the farm. So his father shared his property between his two sons; the younger son packed his bags and went away. He went to a distant city and had a splendid time going from party to party, drinking and eating and dancing…'

'If he didn't work, he would surely run out of money,' said someone.

'He did,' said Jesus, 'and just when he had run out of money there was a dreadful famine in that land, so the cost of food shot up. He had to sell all his fine clothes and get a job. He found work looking after pigs but still he could not get enough to eat. He was so hungry that he would have eaten the pea pods and vegetable scraps the pigs had, but no one let him eat even that.

'Then he thought, "Why don't I go home? My father's hired workers have enough food to fill themselves, with leftovers they could give away. He probably won't want me back after what I've done, but if I ask him to take me on as a hired worker, at least I will have enough to eat."

'So he set off and trudged the long, weary road home. As he got closer, he got more and more scared. He rehearsed speech after speech but felt sick imagining what his father might say.

'But all through the years the young man had been away – and never sent a letter – his father had hoped and dreamed that his son would come home. He often looked down the road and

imagined his boy striding towards him. That day, he could hardly believe his eyes – his son was really there, but he was limping, not striding. At once, he rushed down the road to meet him.

'"Father," began the young man, "I've hurt you and I'm not fit to be your son, but please just treat me like one of your hired workers and…"

'But his father hugged him and kissed him before he could finish what he had rehearsed saying.

'"Here," his father called to the astonished servants, "get the best clothes for my son, and some decent sandals. And prepare the best food. We'll have a barbecue – a whole calf. A feast for everyone. And tell his mother – she will be so pleased. My son is back. We thought he might be dead, but he's alive. Let's have a party!"

'Later, the older son trudged wearily home after a hard day's work in the fields. He heard the noise of music and dancing.

' "What is going on?" he demanded.

' "Your younger brother has come home so we are having a party," replied a servant.

'The older son was furious and refused to join the fun. His father came out and begged him to come in.

' "It's not fair, Father," he complained. "I have obeyed your every instruction. I have worked for you for years and years and never had even a small party with my friends. And now that lazy, selfish, disobedient brother of mine has come home and you have given him the best of everything."

' "My dear son,' his father said, 'everything I have is yours. If you wanted a party, you had only to say. But your brother was lost and he's now found. We all thought he might be dead, but he's alive and well. So please be glad and join in the party."'

The Widow and the Judge

Jesus says not to get discouraged in asking things of God.

THE DISCIPLES WERE feeling rather gloomy.
'Sometimes,' Peter confessed to Jesus, 'it feels as if God just doesn't listen. I mean, we pray and pray but nothing changes.'

'Or things get worse,' said Thomas.

'Don't be discouraged or lose hope,' said Jesus. 'Listen to this story:

'There was once a judge. His job was to settle all the quarrels that people could not sort out themselves. He had to listen to everyone involved and decide who was right, who was wrong and what was fair.'

Peter was still feeling gloomy. 'There are some judges whom people can pay to decide what you want so you win your case – no fairness in that!'

'Yes,' said Jesus, 'there are. In fact, this judge did not respect God nor cared what anyone thought of him.

'There was also a widow living in the same town. She was having a hard time – a neighbour had cheated her out of some money but, because she was just a poor woman, he didn't care. She could not afford to pay the judge to decide she was in the right, even though she was. But she was a stubborn woman. She was determined to get her money back. She went to the judge and boldly made her claim: "Sir, give me justice. Make my neighbour give me back my money."

'The judge looked at her as if she were a piece of dirt. "Don't waste my time. Go back to whatever gutter you came from."

'But the woman would not leave him alone. Every time he went out into the street, she'd be there calling to him, "Sir, give me justice."

'He went to visit his friends. She was there. "When will I have justice?"

'He tried to sneak home without being seen but there she was, shouting out, "Justice!"

'When he went to the

market, she followed him crying, "Sir, give me justice."

'She was everywhere. She even met him outside the synagogue crying, "Give me justice like it says in scripture: 'Let justice flow like an unending river.'"

'It did not matter how many times he ignored her or told her to go away – she still kept bothering him.

'Eventually he said to himself, "I do not respect God nor care what other people think of me, but I am totally fed up with this

wretched woman nagging on and on and on. The only way to stop her is to give her what she wants." '

'So she got her money back,' said Peter.

'Yes,' said Jesus, 'but do you understand the story? Even a bad judge will give you justice if you persist. But God is good — if you keep on praying, God will hear you. You won't really have to wait long, though it might feel like a long time — but you must trust God.'

The Unforgiving Steward

A story about forgiveness.

'WHAT'S THE MATTER?' asked Jesus.

'I'm fed up,' said Peter crossly. 'There are some people who keep bothering me. At first I laughed and told them to stop. But it went on, so I got cross. They keep saying sorry but then they do it again and again. Now I'm not just angry, I'm raging furious! I think I've been patient for long enough. I've forgiven them often enough. Seven times, in fact. I think forgiving someone seven times is more than enough. They can just get lost.'

As Jesus looked at him, Peter felt himself going red.

'I don't think seven times is much,' said Jesus. 'In fact, I think you should forgive someone seventy times seven.

'There was once a king who lent money to his servants so that they could do the work he needed them to do: the weaver to buy thread, the fisherman to buy nets, and so on. They were all expected to make a profit for him.

'One day, the king decided to find out who owed what. The servant who was in charge of the accounts showed him his record of the money.

' "Now, this man – your steward," he said, "owes you 10,000 gold coins."

' "That's a lot of money," exclaimed the king. "In fact, that's a fortune. I'd like it back."

'The steward was sent for and told to pay the king the money.

'He stood before the king and cried, "Your Majesty, I can't pay the money back just now but…"

'"Then when can you pay it back?"

'"Next year," said the steward desperately.

'The king glared at the steward and then turned to the other servants.

'"Sell this steward," the king ordered, "and his wife and his children and all his things, so that I get at least some of my money back."

'But the steward fell on his knees and pleaded with the king, "Have mercy, Your Majesty. Be patient and I will pay you everything."

'The king was a kind man. He felt sorry for the steward.

'"Very well," he said, "you may go. In fact, forget the debt. Make a fresh start."

'The steward was very pleased. But, as he left the king's throne room, he met one of the other servants who owed him a few hundred pennies. He seized him by the throat and snarled at him, "Pay me what you owe me – now!"

'His fellow servant fell down on his knees and pleaded with him, "Have mercy, sir. Be patient and I will pay you everything."

' "No! You shall go to prison until you pay."

'And he threw the man into prison.

'The king's other servants were very upset at this. In fact, they were so upset that they went to tell the king.

'The king was furious and sent for the steward. "You wicked man! You owed me a huge amount and I forgave the lot, so you did not have to pay a penny! You should have shown mercy to the poor man who owed you a small bag of pennies. So I have changed my mind. You shall go to prison until you pay me every one of those 10,000 gold coins."

'And that,' said Jesus, 'is exactly how God will treat you unless you forgive what other people have done to you.'

The Workers in the Vineyard

It is never too late to turn to God.

PETER AND THE other disciples were feeling really pleased with themselves.

'We have followed you and given up everything for you, so what special reward will we get in heaven?'

Jesus shook his head and told this story:

'God's kingdom is like this. There was a rich farmer who needed extra people to work in his vineyard at harvest time. At six o'clock one morning, he went to the marketplace where people wanting work waited to be hired. He found some workers already there.

' "Go and work in my vineyard," he said to them, "and I will pay you the usual daily wage."

'The workers agreed to this so they went to work for him.

'But there was still too much work for the workers he had, so the farmer went to the marketplace at nine o'clock as well and

found more workers with nothing to do – so he hired them too.

' "I will pay you a fair wage," he said.

' "This is our lucky day," they replied and went off eagerly to work in the vineyard.

'The farmer went to the marketplace again at noon and at three o'clock. Each time, he found workers standing idle but eager to work. Each time, he hired them to work in his vineyard. Each time, he promised a fair wage. Each time, the workers said that this was indeed their lucky day.

'At about five o'clock, he went down to the marketplace again. He found still more workers standing around looking miserable as evening approached.

'He asked, "Why are you standing here idle?"

' "Because no one has hired us, sir."

' "I will hire you to work in my vineyard and I will pay you what is right."

' "Thank you," they said. "This really is our lucky day."

'At the end of the day, the farmer said to his manager, "Call the workers and give them their pay. Start with the people who came last and finish with the people who came first."

'The manager started giving the workers their pay. He gave the ones who came at five o'clock a silver coin – the fair price for a full day's work. When the workers who had come early in the morning saw this, they began to dream about how much they might get.

"We have worked all day so I wonder what the farmer will think fair for us," they whispered to each other.

'The manager gave each of them a silver coin – a fair price for a full day's work.'

'But,' said Peter, 'that's mean.'

' "Sir, they grumbled, "it isn't fair. These people over there only did an hour's work but we have worked for twelve hours in the scorching heat. We should get more than them."

'But the farmer said, "No, you agreed to a day's wage and I have given it to you as I promised. Take it and go. Don't complain that I am generous." '

Jesus looked at his friends. 'So you see, God is not just fair. He is generous, for he gives more than what is fair. The last will be treated the same as the first, and the first the same as the last.'

The Foolish Bridesmaids

Be prepared: God may come at any time.

SIMON PETER, the fisherman, said, 'The wind's changing. Maybe there's a storm coming.'

'One day,' said Jesus, 'the whole world will change. There'll be no more bad weather. Everything wrong will be put right. God will come and rule – so there will be no tears, but lots of laughter and smiles.'

'And when will that be?' demanded one of the disciples. 'No sign of it yet.'

'This year, next year, sometime…' began another.

Jesus interrupted his gloomy friends. 'Only God knows. But listen:

'Once there was going to be a wedding. The couple were going to be married in the evening after the day's work was done. The bride was waiting and the feast was ready. The guests were all there and it was time for the bridegroom to arrive. There were

also ten bridesmaids. Their job was to stay outside to meet the bridegroom and his followers and lead him in procession to his bride. It was getting dark when they set out, so they took their lamps with them. Five of the bridesmaids were foolish, and five were sensible. The foolish girls had filled their lamps — it is true — but they did not take any extra oil to refill their lamps with in case of any delay. The prudent girls filled their lamps and sensibly remembered to bring extra oil.'

One of Jesus' friends laughed, 'That was wise. Young men who are having a stag party often make the bridegroom arrive late.'

'Yes,' said Jesus, 'and that was what happened — the bridegroom was late. The girls all waited, and as it got later and later they became tired and fell asleep.

'Suddenly they were startled awake by a shout. "Look! Here is the bridegroom! Come and meet him."

'All the bridesmaids got up and trimmed the wicks in their lamps to make them shine brightly. But by now it was midnight, so the oil in their lamps was low.

'The foolish girls begged the others, "Please, give us some of your oil. Our lamps are going out."

'But the prudent girls shook their heads. "Sorry, but no! We do not have enough for all of us — you had better go and find some for yourselves."

'So the five foolish girls hurried away to get some more oil. While they were gone, the bridegroom arrived. Everyone there

went with him to the wedding party; the door was shut and the wedding began.

'Later, the other bridesmaids came back. They knocked on the door and called, saying, 'Sir! Here we are! Let us in."

'But the bridegroom replied, "You know the rules – you were not part of my procession so you do not belong at the feast."

'So,' said Jesus, 'think about that. Don't be like those foolish girls – be ready to meet God at any time. Nobody knows when that will be.'

The Three Servants

A story about using the gifts God has given.

THE GREAT CITY of Jerusalem glittered like gold on the hilltop. Jesus and his friends were on their way there. His friends whispered among themselves about what would happen when they arrived. 'I think the Master will show everyone who he really is. The saviour we've been expecting for thousands of years. The king of God's kingdom.'

'It will be the end of the world.'

Jesus knew what they were talking about.

'No one but God knows when the end of the world will be,' he said, 'but it will be like this:

'A man was going away for a while and told his servants to look after his money.

'"See what you can earn with it while I am away," he said.

'The master called three servants to give them money. To the one whom he thought best at making money he gave 5,000 gold coins.'

Jesus' friends gasped.

'That's lot of money,' said Peter. 'You could keep a family for years on that.'

'To another servant he gave 2,000 gold coins and to a third he gave 1,000 gold coins. The first servant set to work: buying and making and selling at a profit. Instead of 5,000 gold coins, the servant soon had 10,000.

The second servant also set to work: planting and picking and selling at a profit. Soon, instead of 2,000 coins, that servant had 4,000!

'But the third servant dug a hole in the ground and buried his 1,000 gold coins.

'The servants' master returned and asked his servants for the money. The first showed him the 10,000 coins and the master was very pleased. "Well done, good and faithful servant," he said. "I trusted you with a small thing, so now I shall trust you with big things. Come to my party and we can celebrate together."

'Then the second servant showed him the 4,000 coins, and again the master was very pleased. "Well done, good and faithful servant. You have shown yourself trustworthy with this small thing. You too I can trust with big things. Be happy and come to my party so we can celebrate."

'But the servant who had 1,000 coins said, "Master, I knew you are a harsh man and expect to earn money from another's work. You gather a harvest when others have toiled to sow the seed, so I was afraid of doing the wrong thing. I hid your coins in the ground. Here you have what is yours."

'His master replied, "You wicked and lazy servant. You knew that I expected you to make more money. If you could do nothing else, you could have invested it in the bank so I would get the interest."

'His master said to some other servants, "Take the coins from him and give them to the one with 10,000 coins. When people are lazy and do nothing with what I have given them, I shall take away my gift. So this layabout will not come to my party but be left outside! But people who use what I have given them shall be given more and more."'

About the Parables

The word 'parable' comes from a Greek word meaning 'comparison'. The story is about one thing, but it provides a comparison with something else. Jesus' parables are about everyday situations, but the attentive listener will discover comparisons with what it means to be part of God's kingdom.

The Sower and the Seed

This parable is useful to read through first, because Jesus says why he uses parables and then explains the one he has just told. What happens to the seeds that fall in the different places can be compared to what happens to people who hear Jesus' teaching. People who take Jesus' teaching seriously can make the comparison with themselves: what sort of listener am I?

The Rich Fool

Throughout the Bible are many warnings about the dangers of trusting in money. This simple story shows why: being rich is not what makes a life worthwhile. Notice how often the ultra-rich of today say that money isn't the most important thing. So what is important?

The Great Feast

Respectable, hardworking, successful people have so many worthwhile things to do. However, this parable shows that the most important thing of all is to come to God's kingdom… and God welcomes those who simply come as they are.

The Lost Coin

In many parts of the Bible and in other parables, God is compared to a king or a judge. In this heart-warming parable, God is compared to a diligent housewife. The lost coin that is found is like the person who has done wrong but then wants to obey God. They are greeted not with a telling off but a party.

The Prodigal Son

A prodigal is someone who squanders their money, and the word is most famous for having been the traditional name of the parable (it is not a word Jesus used!). It is a heartening reminder for all young people that going off the rails is not the end. A loving parent will rush to forgive them. So, says the parable, will God. As in The Lost Coin, the welcome home is celebrated.

The Widow and the Judge

This parable can seem puzzling. The pestering widow can be compared to the person who prays and prays but gets no result. So is God like a judge who doesn't care? Not really: the story shows that if persistence can wear down a heartless judge, then a loving God is bound to answer faithful prayer.

The Unforgiving Steward

One of Jesus' clearest messages is that his followers must forgive others. Only then, he says, will God forgive them. This parable shows that people want to be forgiven but are less willing to forgive. How quickly they forget their own wrongdoing!

The Workers in the Vineyard

The employer in this story is entirely fair: he pays everyone what was agreed. By comparison, everyone who becomes part of God's kingdom will receive the same blessing. There is no place for jealousy.

The Foolish Bridesmaids

What time would the bridegroom arrive? Would he be late… like so many! Just as a bridegroom's arrival could not be predicted with certainty, no one knows when the time will come that brings them face to face with God. They need reserves of energy to live as God wants for all the time they are waiting.

The Three Servants

Some people seem to have a head start when it comes to being successful. Whatever a person has been given, it is their responsibility to use it wisely.